Tattoo

Placement

Theme

Planned Date

Palette

Plac

Design

Detail 1

Detail 2

Notes

Tattoo

Placement

Theme

Planned Date

Placement

Palette

Design

Detail 1

Detail 2

Notes

Tattoo

Placement

Theme

Planned Date

Palette

Placement

Design

Detail 1

Detail 2

Notes

Tattoo

Placement

Theme

Planned Date

Palette

Placement

Design

Detail 1

Detail 2

Notes

Tattoo

Placement

Theme

Planned Date

Palette

Placement

Design

Detail 1

Detail 2

Notes

Tattoo

Placement

Theme

Planned Date

Placement

Palette

Design

Detail 1

Detail 2

Notes

Tattoo

Placement

Theme

Planned Date

Palette

Placement

Design

Detail 1

Detail 2

Notes

Tattoo

Placement

Theme

Planned Date

Palette

Placement

Design

Detail 1

Detail 2

Notes

Tattoo

Placement

Theme

Planned Date

Palette

Placement

Design

Detail 1

Detail 2

Notes

Tattoo

Placement

Theme

Planned Date

Placement

Palette

Design

Detail 1

Detail 2

Notes

Tattoo

Placement

Theme

Planned Date

Palette

Placement

Design

Detail 1

Detail 2

Notes

Tattoo

Placement

Theme

Planned Date

Palette

Placement

Design

Detail 1

Detail 2

Notes

Tattoo

Placement

Theme

Planned Date

Placement

Palette

Design

Detail 1

Detail 2

Notes

Tattoo

Placement

Theme

Planned Date

Palette

Placement

Design

Detail 1

Detail 2

Notes

Tattoo

Placement

Theme

Planned Date

Palette

Placement

Design

Detail 1

Detail 2

Notes

Tattoo

Placement

Theme

Planned Date

Placement

Palette

Design

Detail 1

Detail 2

Notes

Tattoo

Placement

Theme

Planned Date

Placement

Palette

Design

Detail 1

Detail 2

Notes

Tattoo

Placement

Theme

Planned Date

Palette

Placement

Design

Detail 1

Detail 2

Notes

Tattoo

Placement

Theme

Planned Date

Palette

Placement

Design

Detail 1

Detail 2

Notes

Tattoo

Placement

Theme

Planned Date

Palette

Placement

Design

Detail 1

Detail 2

Notes

Tattoo

Placement

Theme

Planned Date

Placement

Palette

Design

Detail 1

Detail 2

Notes

Tattoo

Placement

Theme

Planned Date

Palette

Placement

Design

Detail 1

Detail 2

Notes

Tattoo

Placement

Theme

Planned Date

Palette

Placement

Design

Detail 1

Detail 2

Notes

Tattoo

Placement

Theme

Planned Date

Palette

Placement

Design

Detail 1

Detail 2

Notes

Tattoo

Placement

Theme

Planned Date

Palette

Placement

Design

Detail 1

Detail 2

Notes

Tattoo

Placement

Theme

Planned Date

Placement

Palette

Design

Detail 1

Detail 2

Notes

Tattoo

Placement

Theme

Planned Date

Palette

Placement

Design

Detail 1

Detail 2

Notes

Tattoo

Placement

Theme

Planned Date

Placement

Palette

Design

Detail 1

Detail 2

Notes

Tattoo

Placement

Theme

Planned Date

Placement

Palette

Design

Detail 1

Detail 2

Notes

Tattoo

Placement

Theme

Planned Date

Palette

Placement

Design

Detail 1

Detail 2

Notes

Tattoo

Placement

Theme

Planned Date

Palette

Placement

Design

Detail 1

Detail 2

Notes

Tattoo

Placement

Theme

Planned Date

Palette

Placement

Design

Detail 1

Detail 2

Notes

Tattoo

Placement

Theme

Planned Date

Placement

Palette

Design

Detail 1

Detail 2

Notes

Tattoo

Placement

Theme

Planned Date

Placement

Palette

Design

Detail 1

Detail 2

Notes

Tattoo

Placement

Theme

Planned Date

Palette

Placement

Design

Detail 1

Detail 2

Notes

Tattoo

Placement

Theme

Planned Date

Palette

Placement

Design

Detail 1

Detail 2

Notes

Tattoo

Placement

Theme

Planned Date

Palette

Placement

Design

Detail 1

Detail 2

Notes

Tattoo

Placement

Theme

Planned Date

Placement

Palette

Design

Detail 1

Detail 2

Notes

Tattoo

Placement

Theme

Planned Date

Palette

Placement

Design

Detail 1

Detail 2

Notes

Tattoo

Placement

Theme

Planned Date

Palette

Placement

Design

Detail 1

Detail 2

Notes

Tattoo

Placement

Theme

Planned Date

Palette

Placement

Design

Detail 1

Detail 2

Notes

Tattoo

Placement

Theme

Planned Date

Palette

Placement

Design

Detail 1

Detail 2

Notes

Tattoo

Placement

Theme

Planned Date

Palette

Placement

Design

Detail 1

Detail 2

Notes

Tattoo

Placement

Theme

Planned Date

Palette

Placement

Design

Detail 1

Detail 2

Notes

Tattoo

Placement

Theme

Planned Date

Palette

Placement

Design

Detail 1

Detail 2

Notes

Tattoo

Placement

Theme

Planned Date

Palette

Placement

Design

Detail 1

Detail 2

Notes

Tattoo

Placement

Theme

Planned Date

Palette

Placement

Design

Detail 1

Detail 2

Notes

Tattoo

Placement

Theme

Planned Date

Palette

Placement

Design

Detail 1

Detail 2

Notes

Tattoo

Placement

Theme

Planned Date

Palette

Placement

Design

Detail 1

Detail 2

Notes

Tattoo

Placement

Theme

Planned Date

Palette

Placement

Design

Detail 1

Detail 2

Notes

Tattoo

Placement

Theme

Planned Date

Placement

Palette

Design

Detail 1

Detail 2

Notes

Tattoo

Placement

Theme

Planned Date

Palette

Placement

Design

Detail 1

Detail 2

Notes

Tattoo

Placement

Theme

Planned Date

Placement

Palette

Design

Detail 1

Detail 2

Notes

Tattoo

Placement

Theme

Planned Date

Palette

Placement

Design

Detail 1

Detail 2

Notes

Tattoo

Placement

Theme

Planned Date

Palette

Placement

Design

Detail 1

Detail 2

Notes

Tattoo

Placement

Theme

Planned Date

Placement

Palette

Design

Detail 1

Detail 2

Notes

Tattoo

Placement

Theme

Planned Date

Palette

Placement

Design

Detail 1

Detail 2

Notes

Tattoo

Placement

Theme

Planned Date

Palette

Placement

Design

Detail 1

Detail 2

Notes

Tattoo

Placement

Theme

Planned Date

Palette

Placement

Design

Detail 1

Detail 2

Notes

Tattoo

Placement

Theme

Planned Date

Palette

Placement

Design

Detail 1

Detail 2

Notes

Tattoo

Placement

Theme

Planned Date

Palette

Placement

Design

Detail 1

Detail 2

Notes

Tattoo

Placement

Theme

Planned Date

Placement

Palette

Design

Detail 1

Detail 2

Notes

Tattoo

Placement

Theme

Planned Date

Palette

Placement

Design

Detail 1

Detail 2

Notes

Tattoo

Placement

Theme

Planned Date

Palette

Placement

Design

Detail 1

Detail 2

Notes

Tattoo

Placement

Theme

Planned Date

Palette

Placement

Design

Detail 1

Detail 2

Notes

Tattoo

Placement

Theme

Planned Date

Palette

Placement

Design

Detail 1

Detail 2

Notes

Tattoo

Placement

Theme

Planned Date

Palette

Placement

Design

Detail 1

Detail 2

Notes

Tattoo

Placement

Theme

Planned Date

Palette

Placement

Design

Detail 1

Detail 2

Notes

Tattoo

Placement

Theme

Planned Date

Palette

Placement

Design

Detail 1

Detail 2

Notes

Tattoo

Placement

Theme

Planned Date

Palette

Placement

Design

Detail 1

Detail 2

Notes

Tattoo

Placement

Theme

Planned Date

Palette

Placement

Design

Detail 1

Detail 2

Notes

Tattoo

Placement

Theme

Planned Date

Palette

Placement

Design

Detail 1

Detail 2

Notes

Tattoo

Placement

Theme

Planned Date

Palette

Placement

Design

Detail 1

Detail 2

Notes

Tattoo

Placement

Theme

Planned Date

Palette

Placement

Design

Detail 1

Detail 2

Notes

Tattoo

Placement

Theme

Planned Date

Palette

Placement

Design

Detail 1

Detail 2

Notes

Tattoo

Placement

Theme

Planned Date

Palette

Placement

Design

Detail 1

Detail 2

Notes

Tattoo

Placement

Theme

Planned Date

Placement

Palette

Design

Detail 1

Detail 2

Notes

Tattoo

Placement

Theme

Planned Date

Palette

Placement

Design

Detail 1

Detail 2

Notes

Tattoo

Placement

Theme

Planned Date

Placement

Palette

Design

Detail 1

Detail 2

Notes

Tattoo

Placement

Theme

Planned Date

Placement

Palette

Design

Detail 1

Detail 2

Notes

Tattoo

Placement

Theme

Planned Date

Placement

Palette

Design

Detail 1

Detail 2

Notes

Tattoo

Placement

Theme

Planned Date

Palette

Placement

Design

Detail 1

Detail 2

Notes

Tattoo

Placement

Theme

Planned Date

Palette

Placement

Design

Detail 1

Detail 2

Notes

Tattoo

Placement

Theme

Planned Date

Palette

Placement

Design

Detail 1

Detail 2

Notes

Tattoo

Placement

Theme

Planned Date

Placement

Palette

Design

Detail 1

Detail 2

Notes

Tattoo

Placement

Theme

Planned Date

Palette

Placement

Design

Detail 1

Detail 2

Notes

Tattoo

Placement

Theme

Planned Date

Palette

Placement

Design

Detail 1

Detail 2

Notes

Tattoo

Placement

Theme

Planned Date

Palette

Placement

Design

Detail 1

Detail 2

Notes

Tattoo

Placement

Theme

Planned Date

Palette

Placement

Design

Detail 1

Detail 2

Notes

Tattoo

Placement

Theme

Planned Date

Palette

Placement

Design

Detail 1

Detail 2

Notes

Tattoo

Placement

Theme

Planned Date

Palette

Placement

Design

Detail 1

Detail 2

Notes

Tattoo

Placement

Theme

Planned Date

Placement

Palette

Design

Detail 1

Detail 2

Notes

Tattoo

Placement

Theme

Planned Date

Placement

Palette

Design

Detail 1

Detail 2

Notes

Tattoo

Placement

Theme

Planned Date

Palette

Placement

Design

Detail 1

Detail 2

Notes

Tattoo

Placement

Theme

Planned Date

Palette

Placement

Design

Detail 1

Detail 2

Notes

Tattoo

Placement

Theme

Planned Date

Palette

Placement

Design

Detail 1

Detail 2

Notes

Tattoo

Placement

Theme

Planned Date

Placement

Palette

Design

Detail 1

Detail 2

Notes

Tattoo

Placement

Theme

Planned Date

Palette

Placement

Design

Detail 1

Detail 2

Notes

Tattoo

Placement

Theme

Planned Date

Palette

Placement

Design

Detail 1

Detail 2

Notes

Tattoo

Placement

Theme

Planned Date

Placement

Palette

Design

Detail 1

Detail 2

Notes

Tattoo

Placement

Theme

Planned Date

Palette

Placement

Design

Detail 1

Detail 2

Notes

Tattoo

Placement

Theme

Planned Date

Palette

Placement

Design

Detail 1

Detail 2

Notes

Tattoo

Placement

Theme

Planned Date

Palette

Placement

Design

Detail 1

Detail 2

Notes

Tattoo

Placement

Theme

Planned Date

Palette

Placement

Design

Detail 1

Detail 2

Notes

Tattoo

Placement

Theme

Planned Date

Palette

Placement

Design

Detail 1

Detail 2

Notes

Tattoo

Placement

Theme

Planned Date

Placement

Palette

Design

Detail 1

Detail 2

Notes

Tattoo

Placement

Theme

Planned Date

Palette

Placement

Design

Detail 1

Detail 2

Notes

Tattoo

Placement

Theme

Planned Date

Palette

Placement

Design

Detail 1

Detail 2

Notes

Tattoo

Placement

Theme

Planned Date

Palette

Placement

Design

Detail 1

Detail 2

Notes

Tattoo

Placement

Theme

Planned Date

Placement

Palette

Design

Detail 1

Detail 2

Notes

Tattoo

Placement

Theme

Planned Date

Palette

Placement

Design

Detail 1

Detail 2

Notes

Tattoo

Placement

Theme

Planned Date

Palette

Placement

Design

Detail 1

Detail 2

Notes

Tattoo

Placement

Theme

Planned Date

Palette

Placement

Design

Detail 1

Detail 2

Notes

Tattoo

Placement

Theme

Planned Date

Palette

Placement

Design

Detail 1

Detail 2

Notes

Tattoo

Placement

Theme

Planned Date

Palette

Placement

Design

Detail 1

Detail 2

Notes

Tattoo

Placement

Theme

Planned Date

Palette

Placement

Design

Detail 1

Detail 2

Notes

Tattoo

Placement

Theme

Planned Date

Palette

Placement

Design

Detail 1

Detail 2

Notes

Tattoo

Placement

Theme

Planned Date

Placement

Palette

Design

Detail 1

Detail 2

Notes

Tattoo

Placement

Theme

Planned Date

Palette

Placement

Design

Detail 1

Detail 2

Notes

Tattoo

Placement

Theme

Planned Date

Palette

Placement

Design

Detail 1

Detail 2

Notes

Tattoo

Placement

Theme

Planned Date

Placement

Palette

Design

Detail 1

Detail 2

Notes

Tattoo

Placement

Theme

Planned Date

Palette

Placement

Design

Detail 1

Detail 2

Notes

Tattoo

Placement

Theme

Planned Date

Palette

Placement

Design

Detail 1

Detail 2

Notes

Tattoo

Placement

Theme

Planned Date

Palette

Placement

Design

Detail 1

Detail 2

Notes

Tattoo

Placement

Theme

Planned Date

Placement

Palette

Design

Detail 1

Detail 2

Notes

Tattoo

Placement

Theme

Planned Date

Placement

Palette

Design

Detail 1

Detail 2

Notes

Tattoo

Placement

Theme

Planned Date

Palette

Placement

Design

Detail 1

Detail 2

Notes

Tattoo

Placement

Theme

Planned Date

Palette

Placement

Design

Detail 1

Detail 2

Notes

Tattoo

Placement

Theme

Planned Date

Palette

Placement

Design

Detail 1

Detail 2

Notes

Tattoo

Placement

Theme

Planned Date

Palette

Placement

Design

Detail 1

Detail 2

Notes

Tattoo

Placement

Theme

Planned Date

Palette

Placement

Design

Detail 1

Detail 2

Notes

Tattoo

Placement

Theme

Planned Date

Placement

Palette

Design

Detail 1

Detail 2

Notes

Tattoo

Placement

Theme

Planned Date

Palette

Placement

Design

Detail 1

Detail 2

Notes

Tattoo

Placement

Theme

Planned Date

Palette

Placement

Design

Detail 1

Detail 2

Notes

Tattoo

Placement

Theme

Planned Date

Palette

Placement

Design

Detail 1

Detail 2

Notes

Tattoo

Placement

Theme

Planned Date

Palette

Placement

Design

Detail 1

Detail 2

Notes

Tattoo

Placement

Theme

Planned Date

Palette

Placement

Design

Detail 1

Detail 2

Notes

Tattoo

Placement

Theme

Planned Date

Placement

Palette

Design

Detail 1

Detail 2

Notes

Tattoo

Placement

Theme

Planned Date

Placement

Palette

Design

Detail 1

Detail 2

Notes

Tattoo

Placement

Theme

Planned Date

Palette

Placement

Design

Detail 1

Detail 2

Notes

Tattoo

Placement

Theme

Planned Date

Palette

Placement

Design

Detail 1

Detail 2

Notes

Tattoo

Placement

Theme

Planned Date

Palette

Placement

Design

Detail 1

Detail 2

Notes

Tattoo

Placement

Theme

Planned Date

Palette

Placement

Design

Detail 1

Detail 2

Notes

Tattoo

Placement

Theme

Planned Date

Palette

Placement

Design

Detail 1

Detail 2

Notes

Tattoo

Placement

Theme

Planned Date

Palette

Placement

Design

Detail 1

Detail 2

Notes

Tattoo

Placement

Theme

Planned Date

Palette

Placement

Design

Detail 1

Detail 2

Notes

Tattoo

Placement

Theme

Planned Date

Palette

Placement

Design

Detail 1

Detail 2

Notes

Tattoo

Placement

Theme

Planned Date

Palette

Placement

Design

Detail 1

Detail 2

Notes

Tattoo

Placement

Theme

Planned Date

Palette

Placement

Design

Detail 1

Detail 2

Notes

Tattoo

Placement

Theme

Planned Date

Palette

Placement

Design

Detail 1

Detail 2

Notes

Made in the USA
Monee, IL
26 April 2021